T0012204

THE LITTLE BOOK OF
TRIATHLON

Published in 2023 by OH!
An Imprint of Welbeck Non-Fiction Limited,
part of Welbeck Publishing Group.
Offices in: London – 20 Mortimer Street, London W1T 3JW
and Sydney – 205 Commonwealth Street, Surry Hills 2010
www.welbeckpublishing.com

ISBN 978-1-80069-409-5

Compiled and written by: David Clayton
Editorial: Victoria Denne
Design: Tony Seddon
Project manager: Russell Porter
Production: Jess Brisley

A CIP catalogue record for this book is available from the British Library

Printed in China

10 9 8 7 6 5 4 3 2 1

THE LITTLE BOOK OF
TRIATHLON

FOR EVERYONE FROM
THE NOVICE TO THE ENTHUSIAST

CONTENTS

INTRODUCTION

Triathlons – three separate and gruelling tests of endurance in their own right, all rolled into one epic test of mind, body, and determination.

Comprising long-distance running, swimming, and cycling, triathlons are the pinnacle of human endurance, taken on by men and women with a burning ambition to push themselves to the very limit.

So, why do triathletes do what they do?

Most often, the answer is to test their own boundaries and discover what they're capable of, and then going again, and again, and again...

The training for a triathlon eats up days, weeks and months, and commitment to the sport is total.

In the pages that follow you will discover inspirational quotes and words of wisdom that will make you smile and reach for your running shoes/swimming gear/cycling helmet with renewed vigour. And along the way, you'll learn need-to-know stuff, some triathlon history and tips from the experts.

As you discover what it really takes to become a triathlete, it might also become your passion.

The Little Book of Triathlon is a journey on a path that is less trodden, but rich in fulfilment, self-discovery and everything in-between.

On your marks, set... and on we go.

CHAPTER
ONE

Need-to-Know Stuff and History

Everything you wanted to know about a triathlon – and plenty more!

Start at the beginning...

So, what is a triathlon? 'A triathlon comprises three different disciplines – swimming, cycling, and running (in that order)'.

Source: humanrace.co.uk

Basically...

The most common triathlon distance follows international Olympic guidelines, which includes:

SWIM 1.5 k

CYCLE 40 k

RUN 10 k

All Greek to me

The word "triathlon" is derived from the Greek words "treis" (three) and "athlos" (sports).

The same formula is used to name sports events involving different numbers of sports, such as pentathlon (five sports) and decathlon (ten sports).

Powerful body

Founded in 1982, USA Triathlon sanctions more than 4,300 events and connects with more than 400,000 members each year, making it the largest multisport organization in the world.

Origins

The first recorded triathlon consisting of a swim/bike/run event was held at Mission Bay, San Diego, California on September 25, 1974.

The race was conceived and directed by Jack Johnstone and Don Shanahan, who were both members of the San Diego Track Club which sponsored the event.

How?

Simon Lessings holds the Olympic distance triathlon world record with a time of 1 hour, 39 minutes, 50 seconds.

The Great Britain athlete achieved this remarkable feat in 1996 in Cleveland, Ohio. That's fast!

When the going gets tough...

Considered one of the most difficult one-day sporting events in the world, the Ironman Triathlon is one of a series of long-distance triathlon races organized by the World Triathlon Corporation and consists of a 3.86 kilometre swim, a 180.25 kilometre bike ride and a 42.20 kilometre marathon.

Everyone's a winner

Most Ironman competitions have a strict time limit of 17 hours to complete the course, but anyone who makes it to the end under the time limit can call themselves Ironman (or woman).

Make mine a Hawaiian

The Ironman World Championship is held every year in Kona, Hawaii over the full-distance triathlon.

The best male and female athletes on the planet compete and the race, which costs just over $1,000 to enter, is open to pros and age groupers through qualification only.

Source: mytriworld.com

Child's play?

According to the British Triathlon Federation, the youngest age that you can compete in a triathlon is eight years old.

The "mini" distances are a 50 m swim, a 800 m bike ride and a 600 m run!

(Fairly) new kid on the block

Despite comprising three of the oldest sports in history, triathlon is a relatively new sport that has taken the world by storm – particularly the United States, where there are approximately 4,300 races each year.

Burn, baby, burn

It's not uncommon for an athlete to burn over 10,000 calories during the race, and on average an Ironman will lose 5.5 pounds during that time as well. That's about five times the recommended caloric intake for the average American – and a great way to stay in shape!

Source: active.com

Pee-wee he-man

If you've ever wondered how a triathlete holds in a visit to the toilet during the race, the answer is...

they don't!

In a sport where every second counts, a bathroom stop might mean the difference between a spot on the podium and fourth place, so triathletes go either in their wetsuits while swimming, on their bike while in the saddle, or on the go while running!

Source: active.com

Age is just a number

In 2018, age-group triathlete Hiromu Inada became the oldest Ironman World Championship finisher. At 85 years old, he completed the 2.4-mile swim, 112-mile bike ride and the 26.2-mile run in 16:53:50...

crossing the line less than seven minutes before the cut-off time. He proved age is just a number, and it's never too late to start. He didn't complete his first triathlon until he was 70, when he was just a kid!

Source: active.com

On the run!

The Escape from Alcatraz triathlon starts with a swim to shore from Alcatraz island, followed by a 29 km bicycle ride and a 13 km run in the San Francisco Bay area, which is renowned for its steep hills and dips. The run includes a section called the "Sand Ladder", which involves scaling a 400-step staircase up a cliff.

Source: escapealcatraztri.com

Must-watch TV

Coverage of the Ironman World Championship on US TV channel NBC is what many triathletes in the States claim to have inspired them to take up the sport. This annual 90-minute programme has won 17 Emmy awards for outstanding edited sports event coverage and has been nominated 55 times since its debut in 1991, recently beating coverage of World Series baseball, UFC, and Super Bowl coverage in 2017.

Source: active.com

Two's company

The original (and possibly only) tandem triathlon is held every year in the small market town of Bishop's Castle in Shropshire, England.

The first event took place in 1986. The athletes compete in teams of two, one of whom is a swimmer and the other a runner.

The race starts with the swimmer completing a 1 km swim, then both members of the team cycle a hilly 35 km route before the runner completes a 10 km run around an Iron Age hill fort.

Both athletes then hop back on the tandem for a 5 km downhill cruise to the finish line.

Olympic rules

An Olympic distance triathlon comprises of a 1500 m swim, a 40 k bike ride and a 10 k run – about the distance from Manchester to Liverpool in the UK. Easy!

There are various discrepancies in types of triathlon – here are the main need-to-know distances:

	Swim	Bike	Run
Sprint	0.5 mi (750 m)	12.4 mi (20 km)	3.1 mi (5 km)
Olympic/5150	0.93 mi (1.5 km)	24.8 mi (40 km)	6.2 mi (10 km)
ITU Long	1.86 mi (3 km)	49.6 mi (80km)	12.4 mi (20 km)
Half/70.3	1.2 mi (1.9 km)	56 mi (90 km)	13.1 mi (21.09 km)
Full	2.4 mi (3.8 km)	112 mi (180 km)	26.2 mi (42.195 km)

Source: totaltriathlon.com

Make a DATE(V)

The DATEV Challenge
in Roth, Germany is held
each summer around
June or July.

A full-distance triathlon,
(3.9 k swim; 180 k bike;
42.2 k run), this event is
the best Ironman distance
triathlon around for a PB
(personal best).

It holds the world record for the fastest times at this distance for both men and women (Jan Frodeno 07:35:39 and Chrissie Wellington 08:18:13, respectively). It's also the biggest triathlon event in the world, boasting nearly 5,000 athletes in total (including relay) and over 250,000 spectators.

Source: letsdothis.com

World's toughest triathlon?

The SavageMan Triathlon Festival, held each year at Deep Creek Lake in Maryland, is known for its hills and naturally occurring course challenges.

In fact, the SavageMan 70.0 Triathlon is widely considered the toughest half–ironman distance triathlon in the world due to its severe climbing.

But it's not all bad - that is just the SavageMan 70.0.

Less well known is that the SavageMan Olympic distance triathlon, the SavageMan 30.0, is a far less extreme course. And even less well known than that is the SavageMan Sprint distance triathlon, the SavageMan 20.0, which is not at all hilly and is legitimately a flat and fast course.

GOLDEN RULES

Swimming

Any swim stroke is permitted, and you can switch whenever you want at any time.

You can even tread water or float if you need to stop and rest or adjust your swimsuit or goggles.

Holding onto an inanimate object such as a boat or buoy is also permitted – as is standing if the water is shallow enough – but you can't use them to push off and gain an advantage.

Flippers, swim gloves, floaties or any sort of propulsion device is not permitted, though goggles may be worn.

GOLDEN RULES

Biking

Helmet first! You are not allowed to mount your bike until your helmet is on and secured.

Should you have an accident or render your bike inoperable, you are allowed to push or carry it to the finish line – but you can't move forward without the bike.

Unlike typical time-trial bike riding, drafting is not allowed in triathlons. Once you enter the draft zone of the biker in front of you, you have 15 seconds to either pass or fall back. Failing to do so will result in a time penalty being assessed.

GOLDEN RULES

Running

You can't literally crawl over the finish line!

Injury or other reasons for prevention of running or walking mean leaving the marked course until you can continue or are forced to retire.

There are very few running rules, as no additional equipment is required.

Body marking

Body marking happens during race check in. It is when information such as race number and age are written on athletes' upper arms and calves to assist race officials during an event.

Source: totaltriathlon.com

GOLDEN RULES
Transitions

Cycling speed must remain low when exiting the Transition 1 (T1) area and entering the Transition 2 (T2) area.

A physical mount and dismount line will separate the transition area and the biking course. Those two will be placed at a different location in most races, so it's worth checking those before the race.

Equipment – including clothing and bikes – must be put only in the designated areas. Bikes must be placed in the upright position in the bike corral.

And most important of all: stay out of other people's way and remember – a tidy ship is a happy one!

CHAPTER
TWO

The Great and the Good

There are many triathletes who have made their name in the sport and been a source of inspiration for thousands of others.

Here's the thoughts of some of them...

"

The run's the business end of
a triathlon: it's where you win
or lose the race. I like to get out
very hard, make other people
hurt sometimes, and other times
leave it to the last kilometre and
really win the race there. You
shouldn't eat anything new on
race days. Eat simple foods, and
ones that you can easily digest.

"

Alistair Brownlee

*Olympic gold medallist for Great Britain in
2012 and 2016*

"

I knew I had trained very well, but these guys who were with me at the front were really the big guys. I just tried to execute my own race. As Simon [Whitfield] went, I knew it was going to be tough. I just had to bite and fight.

"

Jan Frodeno

The man considered by many to be one of the greatest triathletes of all time, on his gold medal triumph at the 2008 Olympic Games

"

I saw Jonny start to veer off to the side and I thought: 'He's not looking good.' I ran towards him, grabbed him, and started dragging him towards the finish line, hurling profanities at him all the way.

"

Alistair Brownlee

Alistair reflects on the time he elected to help his younger brother Jonny rather than race towards victory in a dramatic end to the World Triathlon Series in Cozumel, Mexico

"

I couldn't yell back – I was just trying to breathe! My first thought was: 'Oh, just leave me alone.' But I couldn't do anything about it.

"

Jonny Brownlee

"

First I was just thinking:
'What an idiot. He could
have won this race so
easily and he's been
tactically so ridiculous. It
serves him right really.'

"

Alistair Brownlee

"

If I had sprinted past him, it would have been much worse. Plus, my mum wouldn't have been happy with that.

"

Alistair Brownlee

"

So you nearly died... that was stupid.

"

Ed Brownlee

Text message to brother Jonny, 2016

"

Not how I wanted to end the season but gave it everything. Thanks @AliBrownleetri, your loyalty is incredible.

,,

Jonny Brownlee's

Tweet from hospital after the Cozumel collapse

"

You go through dark periods in a race. Everyone does. You have got to stay so strong in your own head if you want to succeed.

"

Lucy Charles-Barclay

The 2021 Ironman 70.3 world champion offers advice on how to be just a little bit incredible

"

I don't want to be remembered
as the guy who looked like
a wobbly horse down the
finishing line, but hopefully for
what I've done in the Olympics
and other good races. At
the end of the day, I'm a
competitor and I wanted to
win the world championship.

"

Jonny Brownlee

66

It was brutal. No shade at all. If you're going uphill, your heart rate goes up and it just doesn't come back down.

99

Jan Frodeno

German triathlete legend reflects on his first Ironman title, 2015

"

Basically, the faster you are, the more you are allowed to spend on equipment without risking dorkiness. For example: Super-slow guy with a bit of a beer belly who doesn't train much but has a super nice bike, wetsuit and cryogenic muscle-freezing chamber is the king of dorkiness.

"

Jesse Thomas

"

Mental toughness is not a black or white thing because it can mean many different things in many different situations. Sometimes mental toughness means that you're able to just get yourself to do that same stuff over and over and over...

that's very boring and very inglorious but will lead to those incredible moments. Swimming, cycling, running. As a triathlete, I had to do the same things over and over and over year after year after year.

"

Mark Allen

"

I can't do this until I'm 50. It makes it even more clear that every time I do Kona, it could be the last.

"

Jan Frodeno

Olympic goal medallist and three-times Ironman champion edges towards the end of a glittering era, 2022

"

I always try to keep in mind
that I do all that training for a
reason, which is to compete to
the best of my ability. You need
to enjoy yourself and just get
into the routine of keeping fit
and enjoying being active. That's
always easier once you've made
friends in the sport.

"

Alistair Brownlee

Sound advice from the British triathlete

66

Nothing is more
inspiring to me than
watching the last
finishers of any distance
race struggle across the
line, legs buckling in
salt-crusted jerseys with
tears in their eyes.

99

Jesse Thomas

"

I train for about 30 hours a week. That's at least four hours every day. I swim at seven most mornings. It's got to be your life. You've got to fit everything around it. If that's all you know and it's what you love to do, then it's got loads of positives as well.

"

Alistair Brownlee

The time-consuming truth about triathlon!

"

Not everybody is going to run a marathon or do a triathlon. It's not necessary to do that to be in good health.

"

Michelle Obama

The former First Lady of the United States suggests a gentle jog might be enough – as cited on Kidadl's "Best Triathlon Quotes"

"

Life is like riding a
bicycle. To keep your
balance you must keep
moving.

"

Albert Einstein

As quoted on lifestyleanytime.com's
"The 5 Tactics of Learning By Doing"

66

Life is like a 10-speed bicycle. Most of us have gears we never use.

99

Charles M. Schultz

The author "Charlie Brown" makes a poignant observation – as cited on Kidadl's "Best Triathlon Quotes"

66

You can't get good by staying home. If you want to get fast, you have to go where the fast guys are.

99

Steve Larsen

The late, great, American triathlete and endurance king – never one to duck a challenge – as cited on Kidadl's "Best Triathlon Quotes"

"

Achieving Olympic success requires more than training, skill, science and technique. It requires belief and trust. It has been a privilege to receive that trust.

"

Malcolm Brown

Olympic Great Britain triathlon coach and coach of Jonny and Alistair Brownlee, after receiving his lifetime achievement award from the International Olympic Committee

"

I will never forget those early
years when Malc coached from
the side of the track still wearing
his suit from work, stopwatch in
one hand and umbrella.

"

Jonny Brownlee

*Acknowledging the contribution of his coach,
Malcolm Brown, after his IOC award*

CHAPTER
THREE

Hints, Tips and Trivia

A collection of the best
basic info, helpful advice and
random bits and pieces from
some of the best sources
out there...

Go short before long

"

When you first start looking to enter a triathlon it is easy to get confused with all the different names and distances. Instead of jumping straight into the deep end and taking part in a Long Distance Race, start short – this helps you learn how a triathlon works, get to grips with transition and helps with that feeling of jelly legs.

"

Source: gotri.org/training

It's all about you...

There are many reasons to "Try a Tri" – and most of them are health-related. You are going to challenge yourself and push yourself to the limit and triathlon does this in three different ways – but whatever your motivation, it has to be about you, because you are the one doing it!

Source: liv-cycling.com

Don't get naked!

There is a good chance that you might not have invested in a fancy tri suit for your first race and will therefore have to do a complete change between the swim and the bike.

Whatever you do, be sure not to drop that towel. Nudity of any kind at transition, even if it's accidental, will result in disqualification.

Source: redbull.com

"

No panic training. It's not like sitting an exam, so cramming can't be done the night before. Before the event, the volume of your training should be reduced, but keep the body engaged, with some shorter efforts close to your planned race-day exertion. Carb loading isn't essential, overeating not required. A glass – not a bottle – of wine is allowed, and can settle nerves.

"

Cat Benger

Triathlon coach

Be prepared!

Don't leave anything to chance – final checks should include knowing how to reach the race venue, checking the weather forecast to be sure you have ample kit: and reading the race instructions to absorb the information. And don't bank on sleeping soundly the night before, but make sure you set a reliable alarm (or two) to wake you in plenty of time.

Source: 220triathlon.com

Get Comfortable With Open-Water Swimming

Make sure you know how to swim, especially in open water. Swimming in the pool is one thing, but swimming in open water is a completely different skill for someone new to triathlon. Make sure you get to a body of water with a friend and try swimming in open water well before race day.

Source: trainingpeaks.com

Fuel your body

To compete in a triathlon, you need to treat your body like an F1 racing car – you need the right fuel to fire your cylinders. So, 2 to 3 hours before the race, why not eat:

- toast or bagel with peanut butter

- sliced banana and honey

- coffee

Just 15 minutes before the race, take some kind of energy gel with caffeine (some have caffeine; others don't) and then do so again every 45 minutes while racing.

Source: steadyfoot.com

Pre-race research

It's always a good idea to practice with your nutrition before race day.

Whenever you work out for longer than 50–60 minutes, practice your nutrition plan during your workout, as well as before and after. You will want to find out what foods, energy supplements and protein powders work best for you.

Source: everydayhealth.com

Transition Area

The transition area is the place where athletes keep their equipment needed for the race. Typically, races will have one transition area stocked with racks for your bike on a first-come, first-serve basis for selecting your spot within the area. After each leg of the race, athletes return to transition area to swap equipment and head back onto the race course.

Source: totaltriathlon.com

Shift into gear

The cycling discipline of any triathlon is key to getting the kind of finishing times you are targeting – but how well do you know the course?

Some courses are flat, and others have steep hills straight out of transition.

Make sure your bike is in an easy gear, so you are not having to crank too hard right from the beginning. It's much easier to start easy and shift into harder gears than the reverse.

Knowing the course and knowing which gear you should start in can make the world of difference – don't stall and fall because you didn't do your homework!

Source: liv-cycling.com

Pedal to the metal

Learn how to smoothly get your feet in and out of your bike pedals. Your shoes are clipped in, so when you slow down and try to take your feet out, you'll likely lose your balance and fall – by loosening the tension on the back of the pedals, your feet will come out easier and you should avoid an embarrassing slow-motion fall!

Source: runnersworld.com

List essentials

Write yourself a list of all the equipment you will need to pack for the race.

This will help for your very first triathlon and for every race thereafter. There are so many pieces to the puzzle and even seasoned athletes forget very important items... like a helmet!

Carb intake

Carbs are your major energy source for gruelling workouts, while protein is what your muscles need to help recover afterward.

When training from one to five hours per day, as a general rule of thumb, aim for:

3-8 grams of carbs per kilogram of body weight,

1.5-1.8 grams of protein per kilogram of body weight, and 1 gram of fat per kilogram.

Your carb intake should gradually increase or decrease depending on training intensity and duration.

Technical, but definitely need-to-know stuff.

Source: triathlete.com

Drink it in

Make it a habit to drink several cups of water during your daily routine and try sipping a sports drink while training to help replenish essential carbs and sodium/ electrolytes lost during exercise.

Source: triathlete.com

Size does matter

Your running gear size will not be the same as your cycling gear size – so buy one size up for your cycling apparel. Obviously have a fitting first, but don't assume one size fits all when you are doing a triathlon – remember, you need to be as aerodynamic as possible.

Source: runnersworld.com

Shades of wisdom

You probably won't need sunglasses for your run – and definitely not for your swim – but having them for the cycle discipline is essential for keeping bugs out of your eyes – and of course for sunshine on a bright day.

Source: runnersworld.com

Handy bag

Use carrier bags to get your wetsuit on.

Save wrestling with your wetsuit by putting plastic bags over your feet as you put it on – the ankle sections will slip on much easier as a result and could save you a couple of minutes' prep time! Simple and effective!

Source: runnersworld.com

Lycra is your buddy!

For triathlons, Lycra is your friend. Choose close-fitting Lycra kit to avoid chafing between the thighs so that you will be comfortable for the cycling and running disciplines. Lycra kit doesn't hold water so wearing it under your wetsuit means you'll save time in the first transition.

Source: realbuzz.com

You do you...

Get to know your body and how much hydration you typically need for the duration of time you will be racing. Don't forget to factor in the weather and the humidity!

Source: liv-cycling.com

Bonk

An athelete who has "bonked"
has reached the point where
they can go no further.
Fatique has taken over and
exhaustion has set in.

Source: totaltriathlon.com

Left foot forward

Put your race-timing chip
on your left leg.

Why?

Having it on the right
leg would allow it to get
caught in the bike chain
and cause you to crash.
And that wouldn't
be good...

Source: runnersworld.com

Stack 'em up!

Practicing "Brick" sessions, where you complete two disciplines directly after each other, is the best way to train your body to cope with the demands of changing from swimming to cycling or cycling to running.

Source: realbuzz.com

Just do it...

There is no perfect training plan for your first triathlon. The important thing is to do your best and enjoy the journey of figuring out how to swim, bike and run. How many days can you actually train per week? To start, try to run, bike or swim twice per week. See how that goes and go from there.

Source: liv-cycling.com

"

I also realize that winning doesn't always mean getting first place; it means getting the best out of yourself.

"

Meb Keflezighi

The American marathon runner on keeping expectations realistic – as cited on verywellfit.com's "50 Motivational Quotes About Running"

66

With swimming, I guess
you could say you're staring
at a black line, but I've learned
to have quite a passion for
finding cool pools in all parts
of the world.

99

Sam Long,

as cited on 220triathlon.com (2022)

CHAPTER
FOUR

Quote, Unquote...

Some of the greatest names in triathlon – and those who know the sport intimately – speak. Here's what they said and why...

"

Follow your dreams, believe in yourself and work hard for what you want to achieve, even in difficult times. It will be worth it.

"

Nicola Spirig

London 2012 Olympic champion

66

You go through
dark periods in a race.
Everyone does.
You have got to stay
so strong in your own
head if you want
to succeed.

99

Lucy Charles-Barclay

2021 Ironman 70.3 world champion

66

You can have results or excuses, but not both.

99

Anon

"

Race-morning nerves
are so ubiquitous
in tri, I'm surprised
they're not listed as
their own race-day
discipline.

"

Susan Lake

New Zealand triathlete reveals her start-line jitters

66

Your confidence is fuelled
by what you tell yourself,
and by creating positive
affirmation to reframe your
doubtful thinking can increase
confident thoughts and actions
to help you on race day. I can
do this, and I will do this.

99

Seth Rose

*Mental performance consultant and founder of
Southern California-based Transition Performance*

The faster you run, the sooner you're done.

Anon

"

I'd quit racing tri's, but I need the T-shirts since they're most of my wardrobe.

"

Anon

"

How about a
different kind of
threesome?

"

Anon

"

Swimming, biking, and running all seem so simple, but put them together, throw in the space in between...

and the gear
requirements can
start to look like
a month-long trek
up Everest.

Chris Foster

*Former US National Team triathlete breaks
down what a triathlon is really like*

"

For some sports you need a ball, for triathlon you need two!

"

Anon

> ❝
> I believe we need to make the best from what we have available and be grateful. Use creativity.
> ❞

Antonio Ferreira Da Silva Neto

US Triathlon level 1 coach

"

Real food in its natural state is higher in the naturally occurring vitamins and minerals needed to keep the body functioning at its best when training hard.

"

Marni Sumbal

Sports dietitian, author and Ironman athlete shares some sound nutritional advice

"

It is all right to have the butterflies in your stomach, but you want to get them to fly in formation.

"

Seth Rose

US triathlon coach on harnessing nervous energy into the butterfly effect

"

The race is won by the rider who can suffer the most.

"

Eddy Merckx

Belgian cyclist – one of the world's greatest – with advice any triathlete can take into their cycling discipline – as cited on Kidadl's "Best Triathlon Quotes"

"

It never
gets easier,
you just get
faster.

"

Greg LeMond

American road racer and entrepreneur – as cited on
Kidadl's "Best Triathlon Quotes"

"

That triathlon isn't going to train for itself.

"

Anon

"

Triathletes do not
need to train perfectly,
triathletes need to train
continually.

"

Anon

Race Omaha slogan

CHAPTER
FIVE

Ironmen and Women

The best of the best tell
it like it is...

"

You can keep going and your legs might hurt for a week, or you can quit, and your mind will hurt for a lifetime.

"

Mark Allen

Six-time Ironman world champion – he knows what he's talking about!

66

Continually produce
positive self-talk
to get through the
suffering of triathlon
training and races.

99

Triathlete's Tribe

Source: triathletestribe.com

66
Quitters don't tri. Triathletes don't quit.
99

Anon

One of Race Omaha's many inspirational slogans

66

You don't play triathlon. You play
soccer; it's fun. You play baseball.
Triathlon is work that can leave
you crumpled in a heap, puking
by the roadside. It's the physical
brutality of climbing Mount
Everest without the great view
from the top of the world.

99

Chris McCormack

*Australian triathlete and two-time winner of the
Ironman World Championships tells it like it is, 2018*

66

A winner is a loser
who was willing
to fail and get up, fail
and get up, fail and
get up, fail and get
up and win.

99

Peter Zafra

"

The only easy day was yesterday.

"

Navy SEALS

Elite US military unit motto and one often used by triathletes

"

Races are won or lost in key moments.

"

Chris McCormack

66

You put me in a race
where there's a lot on
the line, especially when
people tell me 'you can't
win', or 'you're too small',
you tell me those things
and I'll find a way to
prove you wrong.

99

Mirinda Carfrae

Australian triathlete and former Ironman

"

I always get asked,
'How fast can
you run?' and the
answer is: 'Faster.'

"

Mirinda Carfrae

66

It's supposed to be hard. If it wasn't hard, everyone would do it... The hard is what makes it great.

99

Tom Hanks

Hanks plays Jimmy Dugan in the movie
A League of Their Own (1992) – a line often used for
inspiration by triathletes

66
If it's hurting me, it's killing them.
99

Sebastian Kienle

German triathlete and 2014 Ironman explains that if he is suffering, his opponents will be suffering more

66

Until you face your
fears, you don't
move to the other
side, where you find
your power.

99

Mark Allen

"

Triathlon doesn't build character, it reveals it.

"

Unknown

"

You can't control outcomes, but process or intent, on the other hand, is where big gains can be made.

"

Gwen Jorgensen

Former Olympic and former ITU world champion, 2014 & 2015

"

The beauty of sport is that it forces you into situations where you must challenge yourself. My best race is the one that hurt the most.

"

Chrissie Wellington

Four-time Ironman world champion shares the secret of her success

"

Success in the sport is, above all else, about enduring suffering.

"

Chris McCormack

*Australian Ironman – never afraid to sugar-coat
life at the top end of the sport*

"

Do the training
you love, remind
yourself why you do
it and hopefully it
will come good.

"

Alistair Brownlee

66

Preparation
is the cornerstone
of confidence,
which in turn is
the cornerstone of
success.

99

Craig Alexander

*Three-time Ironman world champion suggests you can
never prepare too much*

66

Success doesn't mean to win everything, but to make the best out of every situation.

99

Daniela Ryf

Four-time Ironman and five-time 70.3 world champion with an optimistic view on the sport and life

Age groupers

The term age grouper refers to triathletes in the racing communnity who do not hold professional or elite status.

In race events, age groupers will compete among racers in their age groups, which are typically divided up into five-year ranges.

Source: totaltriathlon.com

"

I want to go for it.
I'll be 31 and I have a
sixth and a fourth.
So I feel like this isn't
the point that I can
leave short distance.

"

Marten Van Riel

*The Belgian triathlete on his Olympic ambitions
for Paris 2024*

"

I definitely don't see it as a retirement option.

"

Marten Van Riel

Looking to the future and how seriously he'd take long-course racing once his ITU and Olympic days are over

"

I tore my MCL skiing in my senior year of high school and decided to do an Ironman as my rehab. The rest is history.

"

Sam Long

Multiple Ironman title-holder on making a wise move to triathlon

"

It's been a blur after getting pummelled by a car last week. After feeling and seeing peak fitness in my metrics—after months of work, cancelling Christmas and so much focus—I nearly lost it all.

"

Sam Long

Reflects on getting hit by a car in the build up to the May 2021 Ironman World Championship

66

I love the sport. I love to be outside, see new areas, explore new places and do it in different ways. Sometimes the monotony of one sport can get kind of boring, but with triathlon you can explore the trails, or you can go on your bike.

99

Sam Long

66

When you put yourself
on the line in a race and
expose yourself to the
unknown, you learn
things about yourself that
are very exciting.

99

Doris Brown Heritage

Multi-medal and championship winning athlete

"

Just thought it looked cool, so I cleaned it up and started to use it.

"

Gustav Iden

Norwegian triathlete, crowned the youngest ever Ironman 70.3 world champion in 2019, donned a baseball cap he found during a race that he went on to win, carrying the name of a Taoist temple in Changhua County in Chinese characters

66

It is crazy how I never lost with it, but I think the superpower kind of comes from believing in yourself whether it comes from a lucky hat or a bracelet or whatever.

99

Gustav Iden

On his lucky Taiwanese cap

❝

I'm honestly not a religious man but I'm praying that it goes ahead, October Kona, that would be my dream. If I have one wish left in the sport it would be being in Kona in October and having one more race in peak shape and actually having all the boys there and just having a real rumble in the jungle.

❞

Jan Frodeno

Germany's Olympic gold medallist and his hopes that Kona will remain the spiritual home of the Ironman World Championships

"

The real question that comes to my mind though is what will make the race outside of Kona sing? What will be incorporated into the experience there that leaves the athletes saying, no it wasn't Kona, but it was so amazing and so worth it.

"

Mark Allen

Six-time Ironman champion opines on the decision to relieve Kona, the spiritual Hawaiian home of the Ironman World Championship, of some of its duties after 44 years of hosting

"

I have a lot of rivals, but I think time will always be my biggest rival.

"

Pierre Le Corre

"

For me, it's definitely cycling that I love the most. It's my way of discovering the world.

"

Marten Van Riel

The Belgian triathlete, one of the greatest triathlon one-day performers, reflects on his favourite triathlon disciple

CHAPTER
SIX

The
Finishing
Line

Funny, thoughtful and insightful
– here are triathlon quotes by
competitors, doctors, spiritual
leaders and other sportsmen that
will leave you smiling or pensive
for one reason or another...

"

You can quit if you want, and no one will care. But you will know for the rest of your life.

"

Anon

"

If you set a goal
for yourself and are able
to achieve it, you have
won your race. Your
goal can be to come in
first, to improve your
performance, or just finish
the race. It's up to you.

"

Dave Scott

*Veteran triathlete who dominated Ironman in the
1980s, winning six titles*

"

In triathlon, you don't
get to race that much
so when you're on the
start line you just need
to make sure you focus
on the job at hand and
enjoy yourself.

"

Alistair Brownlee

> ❝
> It's always the athlete's responsibility to check everything. We have to listen to our bodies. Sometimes the hardest part is to back off and rest.
> ❞

Julie Dibens

Great Britain triathlete, 2009 Ironman champion and multi-event winner on the dangers of over-exertion

"

You can continue onward, and your leg will torment you for seven days. However, in the event that you quit, your 'mind and heart'? will sting for eternity.

"

Anon

"

Swim like you're
gonna drown, ride
like you stole it,
and run like they
are chasing you.

"

Anon

"

Triathlon just means I'm not very good at three different sports.

"

Anon

"

Triathletes have the
capacity to propel
their body at high
speeds, through wind
and weather over
long distances. I call
that flying.

"

Anon

"

Failure is a failure only when we stop trying anymore.

"

Sri Chinmoy

Indian spiritual leader whose quotes are often used for inspiration by triathletes

"

If God invented
marathons to keep people
from doing anything more
stupid, then triathlon
must have taken Him
completely by surprise.

"

P. Z. Pierce

*Former Medical Director of the Bloomsday Run in
Spokane, Ironman 70.3 Hawaii, and Assistant Medical
Director of the Hawaii Ironman Triathlon
World Championships suggests triathlons are
somewhat testing!*

"

We are judged by what we finish, not what we start.

"

Anon

66

Triathlon – it's not about finding your limits. It's about finding out what lies just beyond them.

99

Anon

"

It's easy to get caught up in our little world (what?!) of triathlon, talking about the relative dorkiness of specific activities and attire choices. But I've got news for you guys.

According to the 99.9 per cent of the population outside of the sport, we're all big 'ol dorks. The coolest triathlete out there hovers somewhere between captain of the chess club and Steve Urkel on the world scale of coolness.

Don't worry — I don't think it's entirely our faults. It's the nature of our sport, being the outcasts of not one but three more popular and established sports. That's a lot of nerds jockeying for position.

Keith Mills

"

I thought about crocodiles consistently during the swim leg. I was terrified of dying a crocodile death. There were boats on course with guns to help out any competitors suffering attacks.

"

Jodie Swallow

Great Britain 2010 Ironman champion writing on her blog on swimming at Ironman Cairns, 2016

> **"**
> The one time, and only time, I will shush my wife without getting in trouble is at mile 14 of an Ironman Marathon.
> **"**

Trevor Wurtele

Former triathlete competitor turned coach

"

I still have a big problem with confidence if I don't have a good race. It always used to get me down and still does a little.

Now I tell myself to learn from the experience. Everyone has bad days, but you have to move on.

I try to surround myself with positive people.

My family and sponsors are always understanding and supportive whatever happens. There is always another race around the corner to prove yourself.

"

Jacqui Slack

(Great Britain triathlete gives sound advice for anyone in any sport)

"

If you set a goal for
yourself and are able
to achieve it, you have
won your race. Your
goal can be to come in
first, to improve your
performance, or just finish
the race it's up to you.

"

Dave Scott

"

Mike Reilly announced that
I broke the course record, and
where I stood, I looked Mark
Allen straight into his eyes.
So, I said, 'I am so sorry,' and
I apologized, because I really
look up to that man. I was very
much overwhelmed.

"

Patrick Lange

*The 2017 and 2018 Ironman champions after
breaking Mark Allen's 1989 Kona run record with
a 2:39:45 clocking)*

❝

I broke three teeth when I first started training to ride, but it did not make me give up because of fear. I thought if I choose to give up this time, I will have wasted three teeth.

❞

Chia-Chia Chang

Promising Taiwanese triathlete responds to the question of whether she had overcome a significant injury in her young career – the answer is an emphatic yes!

176

"

If your partner decides
to do Ultraman, best you
move out of the house.
Living under a bridge
will probably seem quite
appealing after living
with someone preparing
for an Ultraman. Haha.

"

Guy Crawford

*New Zealand triathlete joking about mood swings
while training hard for the 321-mile Ultraman
Triathlon, 2016*

66

I'm not slow, I'm just enjoying the race longer.

99

Anon

"

Conceive,
Believe,
Achieve.

"

Muhammad Ali

*The mantra that legendary triathlete
Jan Frodeno lives to*

66

Almost drowned,
crashed the bike,
puked on the run.
When's the next Tri?

99

Anon

> ❝
> # The difference between who you are and who you want to be is what you do.
> ❞

Bill Phillips

Winner of the first organized triathlon in the United States in 1974 as quoted on SDSU.com – with some simple but effective advice

66

The miracle isn't that I finished the race. The miracle is that I had the courage to start the race.

99

John Bingham

Ironman triathlete reveals the guts a triathlon demands – as cited on johnbingham.com

"

I'm going to work so
that it's a pure guts
race at the end, and if
it is, I am the only one
who can win it.

"

Steve Prefontaine

*The late American multi-record long-distance runner
with a quote many triathletes can relate to*

"

I've known about, and been enthralled by, Kona as a race for as long as I can remember. Moving the IM World Championships could be seen as undermining that, removing its gravitas and mystique.

"

Alistair Brownlee

Shares his opinion on Kona being forced to share the Ironman World Championship

Elite

Elite triathletes are triathletes who are experienced, highly competitive, and meet the series of qualifications of the particular race sanctioning committee.

Elite triathletes can also be referred to as professional triathletes, and oftentimes have their own wave during competitions.

Source: totaltriathlon.com

"

I'm really, really
proud of this one.
I smiled a few times
when it was just me
and Georgia. I feel
like she brings me
to another level.

We don't really give each other an inch and I just wanted to stay safe because it's super-hot out there.

Flora Duffy

After she secures a fourth triathlon world title and gets the better of Britain's Georgia Taylor-Brown in the Abu Dhabi heat to win a record fourth World Triathlon title

"

When I got a little bit
of a gap on the third
lap of the run it was
a little sooner than
I anticipated but I
thought, 'Well, gotta
go now!'

"

Flora Duffy

*After securing a fourth triathlon world title in
Abu Dhabi, November 2022*

"

I'm really proud of myself
out there today and giving it
everything and doing all I could.
We were battling it out to the
end, and I wouldn't have it any
other way – and I don't think she
would. I'm still learning in every
race, and I still want that world
title one day.

"

Georgia Taylor-Brown

*After agonizingly missing out on the 2022 World
Triathlon title to great rival Flora Duffy*

"

It was really tough, and I was scared of Alistair [Brownlee] because he's a really hard opponent. Thankfully for me, he wasn't great today.

"

Pierre Le Corre

The French triathlete gives an honest verdict of his European championship title win in 2018

"

That suits me better than the Olympic distance because I'm quite hard on pain.

"

Pierre Le Corre

On his gruelling 2022 World Triathlon Long Distance Championships triumph

"

The tragedy of life
doesn't lie in not
reaching your goal.
The tragedy lies
in having no goal
to reach.

"

Benjamin Mays

*Inspirational quote from the US Civil Rights
campaigner often used by triathletes*